seam

Crab Orchard Series in Poetry
First Book Award

seam

TARFIA FAIZULLAH

Crab Orchard Review
& Southern Illinois University Press
Carbondale

24 23 22 21   11 10 9 8

The Crab Orchard Series in Poetry is a joint publishing venture of Southern
Illinois University Press and *Crab Orchard Review*. This series has been made
possible by the generous support of the Office of the President of Southern
Illinois University and the Office of the Vice Chancellor for Academic Affairs
and Provost at Southern Illinois University Carbondale.

Editor of the Crab Orchard Series in Poetry: Jon Tribble
Judge for the 2013 First Book Award: Chad Davidson

Library of Congress Cataloging-in-Publication Data
Faizullah, Tarfia.
[Poems. Selections]
Seam / Tarfia Faizullah.
    pages cm. — (Crab Orchard Series in Poetry)
  ISBN 978-0-8093-3325-7 (pbk. : alk. paper)
  ISBN 0-8093-3325-2 (pbk. : alk. paper)
  ISBN 978-0-8093-3326-4 (ebook)
  ISBN 0-8093-3326-0 (ebook)
I. Title.
PS3606.A39A6 2013
811'.6—dc23   2013028019

Printed on recycled paper ♻

in memory of Tangia

contents

acknowledgments

Many thanks to the editors of the publications in which some of these poems have appeared previously, sometimes in different forms:

The Collagist: "1971"

The Missouri Review: "En Route to Bangladesh, Another Crisis of Faith," "Reading Tranströmer in Bangladesh"

Split This Rock Poem of the Week: "Reading Tranströmer in Bangladesh"

Crab Orchard Review: "Reading Willa Cather in Bangladesh"

Mead Magazine: "Dhaka Aubade"

Blackbird: "Elegy with Her Red-Tipped Fingers," "Aubade Ending with the Death of a Mosquito"

Ploughshares: "Interview with a Birangona 1," "Interview with a Birangona 5"

Mid-American Review: "Interview with a Birangona 2," "Interviewer's Note ii," "Interviewer's Note iii," "The Interviewer Acknowledges Desire," "Interviewer's Note iv," "Interview with a Birangona 6," "Interviewer's Note v," "Interview with a Birangona 7," "Interview with a Birangona 8," "The Interviewer Acknowledges Grief"

The Massachusetts Review: "En Route to Bangladesh, Another Crisis of Faith"

New Ohio Review: "Dhaka Nocturne"

Copper Nickel: "Reading Celan at the Liberation War Museum," "The Interviewer Acknowledges Shame"

Washington Square: "Instructions for the Interviewer"

Poetry Daily: "En Route to Bangladesh, Another Crisis of Faith," "Interview with a Birangona 1," "Interview with a Birangona 5"

Thanks to Paisley Rekdal, who chose "Reading Celan at the Liberation War Museum" for the 2012 Copper Nickel Poetry Prize.

Thanks to my teachers, friends, and colleagues who offered counsel, support, and encouragement, especially Amanda Abel, Craig

Arnold, Neelanjana Banerjee, John Beardsley, Kate Beles, Misha Chowdhury, Matthew Crady, Thom Didato, Laura Davenport, Lawrence-Minh Bùi Davis, Benjamin Dombroski, Gregory Donovan, Claudia Emerson, JB Ferguson, Mary Flinn, Kathleen Graber, Anna Claire Hodge, Shanley Jacobs, Cynthia Grier Lotze, Gerald Maa, Catherine MacDonald, Jamaal May, Durba Mitra, Poulami Roychowdhury, Jennifer Tonge, Susan Settlemyre Williams, David Wojahn, and Jake Adam York.

Thanks for the generous gifts of financial support, time, and community to Virginia Commonwealth University, Kundiman, the Bread Loaf Writers' Conference for a Margaret Bridgman Scholarship in Poetry, the Sewanee Writers' Conference for a Tennessee Williams Scholarship in Poetry, the Kenyon Review Writers' Workshop for a Peter Taylor Fellowship, the Dorothy Sargent Rosenberg Memorial Fund, and the Fulbright Program for a research fellowship.

Thanks also to the remarkable Safina Lohani and the brave women of Sirajganj Mohila Sangstha who shared with me their stories and welcomed me into their homes.

And special gratitude to my family, especially Fahmida Faizullah, Tausif Faizullah, and Dr. A. M. Faizullah, for their love, patience, and innumerable kindnesses.

Everything is near and unforgotten.
—Paul Celan

1971

On March 26, 1971, West Pakistan launched a military operation in East Pakistan against Bengali civilians, students, intelligentsia, and armed personnel who were demanding separation of the East from the West. The war resulted in the secession of East Pakistan, which became the independent nation of Bangladesh. According to Bangladeshi sources, two hundred thousand women were raped, and over 3 million people were killed.

i.

In west Texas, oil froths
luxurious from hard ground
while across Bangladesh,

bayoneted women stain
pond water blossom. Your
mother, age eight, follows

your grandmother down worn
stone steps to the old pond,
waits breathless for her

to finish untwining from
herself the simple cotton
sari to wade alone into green

water—the same color,
your mother thinks, as
a dress she'd like to twirl

I

the world in. She knows
the strange men joining
them daily for meals mean

her no harm—they look like
her brothers do nights they
jump back over the iron gate,

drenched in the scents of else-
where—only thinner. So thin—
in the distance, thunder,

though the sky reflected
in the water her mother
floats in burns bright blue.

ii.

Gather these materials:

      slivers of wet soap, hair

           swirling pond water, black oil.

Amar peet ta duye de na,

      Grandmother says, so Mother

           palms the pink soap, slides

it between her small hands

      before arcing its jasmine-

           scented froth across her

back. Gather these materials:

      the afternoon's undrowned

           ceremonies, the nattering

of cicadas—*yes, yes, yes*—

      Mother watches Grandmother

           disappear into water: light:

many-leafed, like bits of bomb-

    shells gleaming like rose petals

        upturned in wet grass, like

the long river in red twilight—

iii.

1971: the entire world unraveling
like thread your mother pulls

and pulls away from the hem of her
dress. In America, the bodies

of men and women march forward
in protest, rage candling

their voices—in Vietnam, monks
light themselves on fire, learning

too late how easily the body burns—
soon, the men whose stomachs

flinch inward will struggle
the curved blades of their bayonets

into khaki-clad bodies, but for now
they lean against the cool stone

walls of your grandparents' house,
eyes closed as your mother watches

her mother twirl in the pond, longs
to encircle herself in ripples

of light her fingers might
arpeggio across green water—

she loves the small diamond
in her mother's nose, its sunlit

surface glittering like curled
hot metal she knows falls from

the sky, though never before her eyes.

iv.

Why call any of it back? Easy
        enough to descend with your

mother, down
            and down hard
                        stone steps—*how I loved,*
she says, *to watch her—*

            yes, reach

        forward to touch

                    the sun-ambered softness

of the bright sari Grandmother

            retwines around
                    her body—yes,

your eyes
        dazzled by the diamond's

many-chambered light
            —it shined
so, Mother says,
            though it's not you

        she's speaking to anymore,

caught as she is in this reeling
                          backward—1971
         and a Bangladeshi

woman catches the gaze
                          of a Pakistani
soldier through rain-curved palm

              trees—her sari is torn
                                        from her—
She bathed the same
              way each time, Mother says

—the torn woman curls
                     into green silence—*first, she*

would fold her sari,
              then dive in—yes,

the earth green
              with rain, the water,

green—*then she would*
                     wash her face
until her nose pin shined, aha re,
how it shined—

              his eyes, green

—*then she would ask me to wash her back*—

                     the torn woman a helix of blood

—*then she would rub cream into her*
beautiful skin—

8

the soldier buttoning
         himself back

into khaki—yes, call it
         back again—

v.

Two oceans between you, but still
you can see her running a finger
along the granite counter in the sun-

spilled kitchen, waiting for the tea
to boil before she drives past old
west Texas oil fields still bright

with bluebells. *But tell me,* she asks,
*why couldn't you research the war
from here?* Gather these materials,

these undrowned ceremonies—
tea poured into a cup, a woman
stepping lightly across green field

into a green pond—but don't tell
her the country of her birth
became a veined geography inside

you, another body inside your own—*Oh
Maa,* she sobs. *I miss her so.* You open
the door to step out to the concrete

veranda. Look: the moon is an ivory
scythe gutting another pond across
which the reflection of a young girl's

braid ripples. *Tell me,* you say, *about 1971.*

En Route to Bangladesh, Another Crisis of Faith

—at Dubai International Airport and ending with a line by César Vallejo

Because I must walk
    through the eye-shaped
shadows cast by these
    curved gold leaves thick
atop each constructed
    palm tree, past displays
of silk scarves, lit
    silhouettes of blue-bottled
perfume—because
    I grip, as though for the first
time, a paper bag
    of french fries from McDonald's,
and lick, from each fingertip,
    the fat and salt as I stand alone
to the side of this moving
    walkway gliding me past dark-
eyed men who do not look
    away when I stare squarely
back—because standing
    in line to the restroom I want
only to pluck from her
    black sweater this one shimmering
blond hair clinging fast—
    because I must rest the Coke, cold
in my hand, beside this
    toilet seat warmed by her thighs,
her thighs, and hers.

Here, at the narrow mouth
of this long, humid
          corridor leading to the plane,
I take my place among
          this damp, dark horde of men
and women who look like me—
          because I look like them—
because I am ashamed
          of their bodies that reek so
unabashedly of body—
          because I can—because I am
an American, *a star*
          of blood on the surface of muscle.

Reading Willa Cather in Bangladesh

—with lines from *The Song of the Lark*

Things came too fast for her; she had not had enough preparation.

Gray sky to gray
land, the plane noses
down—I am unchanged,

like the mural of brown
faces still trapped
in the concrete frame

bordering the runway.
The plane circles back,
keeps time with a blinking

screen—how, in a country
split from tip to tip by such
black mold, can each bright

eye locked inside the mural
still stare straight ahead,
sideways, or to the sky?

Each map I have seen
of this country obscures:
each blue line, each emerald

inch of land cannot claim
such cloudy veins, these
long porous seams between

us still irrepressible—

I place one foot then the other on each narrow, rusty step to where the concrete floor is rough and raised as a calloused hand. The speakers from the green-domed mosque click on, heralding the start of *adhan,* call to prayer. Other *adhans* start up, overlap like a choral round, surround me with rich, thrumming Arabic. The sun sets past rooftops, lush green trees, women hurrying past lithe, dark men holding hands. Dusk settles. Each window carved into Dhaka's many high-rises begins to flicker with light.

Dhaka Aubade

Outside, too fragile
    not to consider: rebar
puncturing sky, empty
    sweet boxes stacked
into columns, another
    call to prayer loud then
waning. Even this
    mosquito netting boxing
my bed is in danger.
    I wake from some dream
that leaves me doubled
    over in this light cutting
away half my body—
    how can people hurt
each other, go on
    living? Today, I don't
want anything
    to touch me. I dreamt,
Sister, that you were
    resurrected, no longer
bone erasing bone.
    This water lustrous
with so many people's
    shit continues to tunnel,
relentless. How do I love
    as much as I say I do?

Elegy with Her Red-Tipped Fingers

Two weeks ago I crossed two oceans wide as
the funeral processions to your grave:

bearded men continued to thumb plastic
prayer beads beside your sheet-swaddled

body. Grandmother, in Virginia, I cradled
the phone to my cheek and stood over the dark

skillet, waiting to turn over another slice
of bacon to slip into my mouth, knowing

well that that sin, too, like so many others,
would dissolve once I willed it to. *Allah-er borosha,*

I mumbled to your daughter: *It's Allah's will*:
words I knew couldn't fill even that half-filled

suitcase spilled out across hardwood floor: color
of those low, yellow plains of west Texas Mother

sobbed past on her way to the airport, compelling
her body faster towards yours before it disappeared

into its bamboo-bordered grave. Once, I stood
over your other granddaughter's grave while

cicadas hummed the sky clean. Once, I wanted
to be the white wind shirred across any open

field. Once, I lay beside you, a child unmoving,
a body slowly filling with feathers: together

we listened to Grandfather's breathing, labored
against white mosquito netting—and now you

too are dead, two weeks too early. Now, after
another stitch-thin *rickshawallah* pedals

my ocean-tugged body across those severed
Dhaka streets, and after I have slipped into his dark

fingers a few extra takahs, and after I have made
my way past storefronts choked with glittering

stacks of gold bangles, and after another tailor
has slipped from his neck the faded measuring

tape, and after he has pulled it taut across my back,
around my leg—who, if not you, will ask me

to tear free the folded fabric from its paper parcel
to finger its gleaming softness? Who will ask

of me its worth, its weight? I kneel, open another
razor, plastic-capped, from a slowly-emptying suitcase—

lotion, mosquito repellent, tape recorder—items
on a list I drew thick, black lines through. But

it won't be your voice I rewind over, fast-forward
through. It won't be your hair you'll sit beside

the window to rub henna into. It won't be
your red-tipped fingers I'll press a jar into:

small gift you won't have asked me to bring.
It won't be your veins I'll notice, too late: fluvial

ribbons rising stark and sudden through the silk-thin
skin of your hands that won't turn over another page

of newsprint dark with Bangla: language I speak
now to your grieving daughter, this language

the bodies of women were once broken
open for. *Put up your hair,* you will never

again admonish. *Please let me see your lovely face.*

Reading Tranströmer in Bangladesh

—for Meherunnessa Chowdhury

In Grandmother's house,
we are each a room that
must remain locked. Inside
it, a prayer mat carelessly
folded on a low table, as
though hands that once
pressed down on it are not
now below ground. Who
has stripped bare the white
walls of the black velvet
tapestry depicting Ka'bah,
house of God? *I let in
the netherworld. Something
rose from underneath.* I sit,
wait through my cousin's
sobs. This morning, another
sudden loss: a classmate's
death, she says. Sordid
details flare out like sails
of a ship: mother trapped
in an asylum, father weeping,
his son's warm corpse cradled
in his arms, the chicken bone
still lodged in his young throat.
To whom would this not be
an inelegant death—a caught
bone like one of our own?

*

We enter the familiar
city: cloaked nightly
in fog, lightbulbs,
lanterns, blurred gold—
the rumbling traffic
on the highways,
and the silent traffic
of ghosts. I reach
for my mother's
hand like a child. *Here*
hang the years. They sleep
with folded wings. Already
I want to shed each jagged
dirt road, bodies jostled inside
each swerving car, trains
draped with bodies dangling
like writhing vines—

*

The cars, packed tight,
do not move. *I saw*
the image of an image
of a man coming
forward . . . sudden
as starlight, he lifts
an arm: mere bone,
wrapped in brown
skin, stem of an iris
rotting in water. He
taps the glass. I close
my eyes, see the bone
of his arm trapped
in a young boy's throat.

*It is still beautiful to hear
the heart, but often the shadow
seems more real than
the body.* How thin
the seam between
the world and the world:
a few layers of muscle
and fat, a sheet wrapped
around a corpse: glass
so easily ground into sand.

Instructions for the Interviewer

Once, she will say, *I didn't*
know there was a hollow inside

me until he pushed himself
into it. Once, you learned

that inside you was not hollow
but seam: color of the rim of the river

tonguing the long dark shore
of stone: reflection of yourself

an endless ripple in corrugated
metal: width of the silver bangle

circling now her thin, dark arm.
Take the tea she offers. *Once,*

she will say, *I was young,*
like you. Once, you wanted

anyone to fill you with blue
noise. Once, you didn't know your

own body's worth. Put the porcelain
cup down. Let it slide into

the saucer's waiting hollow.

Tell her what happened to you during the war, commands the woman who runs a support group for women raped during the 1971 Liberation War. Seven women, upright in plastic chairs like a row of dolls on a shelf, stare at or away from me, fix their eyes above my head or towards the open door where noonlight spills out into the gray-bricked courtyard upon which a line of crows alight. *Tell her.* Between us, a low table laden with steaming cups of tea, plates of local sweets none of us touch. *My mother and I were rolling out rice flour rotis at dawn as usual for breakfast,* the first of the women begins.

In 1972, the Bangladeshi state adopted a policy to accord a new visibility to the two hundred thousand women raped during the War of Independence by lionizing them as birangonas (war heroines), though they were frequently ostracized by their families and social circles.

1. What were you doing when they came for you?

Gleaming water sweeps over
Mother's feet. Bayonets. Teeth.

My green and yellow Eid sari
flaps damply between two palm

trees. Grandfather calls to me:
mishti maya. Girl of sweetness.

Aashi, I call back. I finish braiding
my hair, tie it tight. I twine a red string

around my thigh. That evening,
a blade sliced through string, through

skin, red on red on red. *Kutta,* the man
in khaki says. It is only later I realize

it is me he is calling *dog. Dog. Dog.*

*2. Where did the Pakistani military take you, and were
there others there?*

Past the apothecary shop, shut
down, burned flat. My heart

seized, I told it to hush. They saw
its shape and weight and wanted

it too. Past the red mosque
where I first learned to touch

my forehead low, to utter
the wet words blown from

my mouth again and again. Past
the school draped with banners

imploring *Free Our Language,*
a rope steady around my throat

as they pushed me toward the dark
room, the silence clotted thick

with a rotten smell, dense like pear
blossoms, long strands of jute

braided fast around our wrists.
Yes, there were others there.

Interviewer's Note

i.

You walk past white high-rises
seamed with mold. Past a child
wading through drowned
rice fields, one pink blossom
tucked behind her ear. Past
yourself rippling a storefront
window. *Victim: (noun), one*
that is tricked or duped. Past
a woman crouched low
on a jute mat selling bangles.
One that is injured, destroyed
under any of various conditions.
Was it on a jute mat that
she gave birth to the baby
half-his or his or his? *Victim:*
a living being sacrificed. Past smoke
helixing from an untended fire.
Past another clothesline heavy
with saris: for hours they
will lift into the wind, hollow
of any bruised or broken body.

3. Would you consider yourself a survivor or a victim?

Each week I pull hard
the water from the well,

bathe in my sari, wring
it out, beat it against

the flattest rocks—*Are you
Muslim or Bengali,* they

asked again and again.
Both, I said, *both*—then

rocks were broken along
my spine, my hair a black

fist in their hands, pulled
down into the river again

and again. Each day, each
night: river, rock, fist—

*the river wanders this way,
breaks that way, that is*

always the river's play.

Interviewer's Note

ii.

You listen to the percussion

of monsoon season's wet

wail, write in your notebook

bhalo-me, karap-me

chotto-shundori—

badgirl, goodgirl,

littlebeauty—in Bangla

there are words

for every kind of woman

but a raped one

4. Were there other women there? Did you get along
with them?

Between us: a dark metal
bucket, our hands touching.

We pulled water together
from the muddy river we

used to sit beside before
we belonged to that smoke-

watered world missing brothers
and husbands and fathers. I ask for

Allah's forgiveness: I didn't know
I would cherish the vermilion

streak she drew into the seam of her
parted hair. I didn't know my body's

worth until they came for it. I held
her as she shook at night: pond water

scored by storm. She held me
as I shook at dawn. Don't you know

they made us watch her head fall
from the rusted blade of the old

jute machine? That they made us
made us made us made us made us?

The Interviewer Acknowledges Desire

Here, on this concrete
sidewalk swelling
      its relentless tide of debris,
in bodies shouldering

past other bodies. Here,
deep in her own body
      pulsing with the *wait, wait,*
wait of the *rickshawallah*'s

persistent pedaling—here,
in this skin-thin filigree
      of dusk settling over this
marketplace in which she

acknowledges desire: this
bouquet of dried twigs a child
      cradles in her arms. This
fruit, overripe, tossed

into rivulets of human
waste. Each night
      she remembers his mouth,
thighs, throat—dreams

she gives herself over to,
the wincing tincture of sweat
      and hunger waking her
nightly. Come back to her

before she says *no,* like this
child who clasps now her small,
       dirty fingers onto her wrist,
asks her for anything. *I have*

nothing, she says, turning over
her hands, holding them
       cupped open like the split
halves of a pried-open shell.

Interview with a Birangona

*5. Who was in charge at this camp? What were your
days like?*

All I knew was underground: bodies piled on bodies,
low moans, sweat, rot seeking out scratches on our thighs,

the makeshift tattoos he carved on our backs to mark us.
Over milk tea and butter biscuits, the commander asks

what it feels like to have dirty blood running through our
veins. There were days we wooed him, betrayed each other

for his attention—now he turns me over on burlap.
Outside, bundles of jute skim the wide river. I turn

my face away. *Kutta,* he says. *You smell.* Tell me what
you know about the body, and I will tell you how

it must turn against itself. *Now I've seen a savage
girl naked,* he says. How my body became an eddy,

a blackblue swirl. *Don't cry,* he says. How when the time
came for his choosing, we all gave in for tea, a mango,

overripe. Another chance to hear the river's gray lull.

Reading Willa Cather in Bangladesh

Together, they lifted a lid, pulled out a drawer, and looked at something. They hid it away and never spoke of what they had seen; but neither of them forgot it.

Each day, I begin

       to disappear into yards

of silk or cotton—

       the one that is me but not

begins to emerge,

       coaxed out by each hand

pressed against me,

       its desire to remember—

cousin, aunt, beggar,

       vendor—then rain, slanting

like sheets flung out,

       hung up—then rooftops, skin-

thin, lightbulbs swaying

       like newspapers clipped

to clothesline after clothesline—

       then smell after pungent smell

rising from gutter to rooftop:

        fruit: rot: spice: body. It is the sea

itself. It belongs and does

        not belong to me. In my room,

I lift lids, pull out drawers,

        measure time by each object

left behind: string: sandal:

        bead. I watch the servant sweep

floors in wide, bamboo-

        bristled arcs, knowing she dressed

in a thatched hut before

        dawn, grasping and tucking the long

veil around her acid-burnt

        face, its countries of new skin. I do

not ask her how. I thank

        her for the cup of tea. I am afraid

to look her in the eye, its dark

        pupil the same shape and size of pearls

wrapped around my neck

        as my hair is teased up, out—I startle

at glimpses of my throat,

my cheek in a mirrored tray—

each soft inch of skin

    fractured by a white-bristled brush,

these leftover tracings

    of pale powder smoothed over

my cumin-dark skin.

iii.

If burnt, she said, *I'll turn to ash,*
and you wondered if she meant, *Who
will touch me as though they never
did?* She said, *When I remember,
my being shatters,* and you thought of dusk
candling into small flames in dark
canteens across the city, flagrant
across faces of beggars, their gaunt,
atrophied arms they set swinging
to garner the little pity the rippling
glimpses of our faces offer through
each tinted, glossy window. *You
tell me,* she said, *am I not also your mother?*

*6. Many of the birangona had children by Pakistani
soldiers. Did you have a child as well?*

Besides, I did not have the right
hands to hold her close. The blood

spilled from within me out onto
the bamboo mat, a red shroud.

Besides, she could not feed at my
breast: unwilling hollow of flesh

veined like our country's many
rivers. My country, yours—was it

hers? She grew whole inside me
like a lychee, my belly a hard shell

broken open by her soft, wailing
flesh. Besides, I did not want his

or his or his child inside me,
outside me, beside me. Never

will she know that I cupped her
head and began to press hard, but

stopped. That I laid her between
cotton and dirt floor, placed the tip

of my finger over her beating heart.

Interviewer's Note

iv.

Today there is no drinking

water today there is no

light today there is only

kerosene the *hmm hmm hum*

of a generator pulsing deep

into the exhausted darkness

you write the word *shame*—

It is possible to live without

memory Nietzsche said but

is it possible to live with it?

The Interviewer Acknowledges Shame

After she has ducked through
    the low-slung metal shack, the war-
raped women she's come
    to visit offer tea drowsy with sweet.
They begin to speak, unlocking
    the desiccated coffins of their grief.
The video camera's lens blinks
    on their dawn-thin faces until daylight
spools itself back into darkness.
    Anything, she says,
you would like to tell me, anything
    you can remember.
She ducks back under
    the clothesline heavy with faded saris
out to the main road. After
    the *rickshawallah* pedals across town
to a small, heat-spattered
    hotel room, she wraps a dark silk scarf
around herself until twilight
    and rubs her eyes
riverbank-raw until she lies
    on the hard narrow bed and begins
to touch herself. After the familiar,
    arched shuddering, she wishes she could
cry, because that, at least, might be
    redemption for each broken body that can't
be restored. She doesn't feel shame's
    dark-circled tightening after waking
to the mirror, dust-webbed, nor
    when she boards the bus

back to the city. Sunlight
        fades the open windows into white
dreams. A child bends down
        to elevate a pink blossom away
from a green field. It's later: when she arrives
        back at a borrowed flat, begins
to strip off travel-pungent clothes
        and smells her own body's resinous
musk. It's when she sits down naked
        at the desk to rewind and fast-forward through
all the pixelated footage of the women's
        kerosened lives. It's when
she begins to write about it in third person,
        as though it was that simple
to unnail myself from my own body.

7. Do you have siblings? Where were they?

On a thin lavender evening
like this one, we sisters sat

and waited until we were only
listening for them to come.

We became these four walls:
corrugated, twilit. On a thin

lavender evening like this one,
we were each other's world

entire: both the wood rose as well
as its tangled stem. When they came

for us on a thin lavender evening
like this one, we tried to pull

each other out of their rifle-black
hands. We tried to scream through

fingers ripe with our own rivers. On
a thin lavender evening like this one,

she was not yet the ripped bandage
the night turned into the crimson

moon under which I did not know
I would stumble gasping, alone.

We had held each other's hands
but did not promise not to let go.

Interviewer's Note

v.

But wasn't it the neat narrative
you wanted? The outline of the rape
victim standing against a many-winged
darkening sky, shadow flurrying across
shadow? *They tossed me into that*
river but the river wouldn't kill me,
she said yesterday—you want
the darkness she stood against
to be yards of violet velvet
your mother once cut into dresses
for you, your sister when she was still
alive. Rewind. Play. Rewind. *They tossed—*
*me—river—me—*you want the splayed heart
of another's hand clasping yours, to know
if cruelty exists, or if it is only love's threadbare
desperation—*river—me—river—me—me—*

The Interviewer Acknowledges Grief

Sister, I waste time. I play
       and replay the voices of these
hurt women flowering

       like marigolds or thistles.
Something lost, forgotten—
       that picture of you, violin

sewn fast to your shoulder,
       bow in one hand poised
eternal. Again, the power's

       gone out—tell me, what is
it to say I miss you? Because
       you won't grow breasts, never

feel desire rippling across you
       like bolts of silk these many
lithe men unshelf daily

       for my choosing. Because you
can't reassure me I have
       the right to ask anything

of women whose bodies won't
       ever again be their own. You
can't blot away this utter, sooted

       darkness. You don't hesitate
when another birangona asks you,
       Do you have any siblings?

For decades, you've been
        so small: a child tapping
on opaque windows. Now,

        through the veranda's black
iron bars, I see you, dark
        silhouette hurrying past,

a bagged red box dangling
        from one slender arm—gift
for a lover or mother. Again,

        the generator shudders me back
into light. Isn't this, Sister,
        what I always said I wanted?

*8. After the war was over, what did you do? Did you go
  back home?*

I stood in the dark
doorway. Twilight. My grandfather's

handprint raw across my face. *Byadob,*
he called me: trouble-

maker. *How could you let them
touch you?* he asked, the pomade just

coaxed into his thin hair
a familiar shadow of scent

between us even as he turned
away. *Leave. Don't come*

back, he said. I walked past his
turned-away back. Past fresh-plucked

lychees brimming
yellow baskets. Past Mother

on the doorstep sifting through rice flour,
refusing or told not

to look up, though the new
president had wrapped me in our new

flag: a red sun rising
across a green field. *You*

saved our country, he said. I said
nothing. The dark rope

of Mother's shaking arm was what
I last saw before I walked away.

No. No. Not since.

Reading Celan at the Liberation War Museum

—Independence Day Celebration 2011, Dhaka

i.

In a courtyard, in these stacks of chairs
      before the empty stage—*near are*
we Lord, near and graspable. Lord,
      accept these humble offerings:

stacks of biscuits wrapped in cellophane,
      stacks of bone in glass: thighbone,
spine. Stacks of white saucers, porcelain
      circles into which stacks of lip-worn

cups slide neat. Jawbone, Lord. Galleries
      of laminated clippings declaring war.
Hands unstack chairs into rows. *The dead:*
      they still go begging. What for, Lord?

Blunt bayonets, once sharp as wind?
      Moon-pale stacks of clavicle? A hand—

ii.

Moon-pale stacks of clavicle a hand
        brushes dust from. *I lost a word*

that was left to me: sister. The wind
        severs through us—we sit, wait

for songs of nation and loss in neat
        long rows below this leaf-green

flag—its red-stitched circle stains
        us blood-bright blossom, stains

us river-silk—*I saw you, sister, standing*
        in this brilliance—I saw light sawing

through a broken car window, thistling
        us pink—I saw, sister, your bleeding

head, an unfurling shapla flower
        petaling slow across mute water—

iii.

Petaling slow
                    across mute water,
bows of trawlers
                    skimming nets
of silver fish that ripple
                    through open
hands that will carve them
                    skin-

less. *We were hands,*
                    we scooped
the darkness empty. We
                    are rooted
bodies in rows silent before
                    the sparked
blue limbs of dancers
                    leafing the dark

light indigo, then
                    jasmine alighting
into a cup, then
                    hands overturning
postcards bearing flag
                    and flower, hands
cradling the replica of a boat,
                    hands

thrust there and into
                    nothingness. You,
a corpse, sister, bathed
                    jasmine, blue—

iv.

A corpse: sister, bathed jasmine. Blue,

                    the light leading me from this gift shop into

a gallery of gray stones: *Heartgray puddles,*

                    two mouthfuls of silence: the shadow

            cast by the portrait of a raped woman trapped

in a frame, face hidden behind her own black

                    river of hair: photo that a solemn girl

your corpse's age stands still and small

                    before. She asks, *Did someone hurt her?*

Did she do something bad? Her mother

                    does not reply. Her father turns, shudders,

as the light drinks our silences, parched—

                    as I too turn in light, spine-scraped—

you teach you teach your hands to sleep

v.

you teach you teach your hands to sleep

because her hands can't hold the shape

of a shapla flower cut from its green leaf

because her hands can't hold grief

nor light nor sister   in her hands fistfuls

of her own hair   on her wrists glass bangles

like the one you struggled over your hand

the same hand that slapped a sister's wan

face   look   the young girl stands before

the photo of the young woman who swore

she would not become the old woman

crouched low on a jute mat holding

out to you a bangle   *a strange lostness was*

bodily present   you came near to living

vi.

Bodily present, you came near to living,
       Poet, in this small blue dress still stained,

the placard states, with the blood of the child
       crushed dead by a soldier's boot. Who failed

and fails?—nights you couldn't bear the threshed
       sounds of your heart's hard beating. I press

a button: 1971 springs forth: black and white
       bodies marching in pixelated rows. Nights

you resuscitated *the Word, sea-overflowed,*
       star-overflown. A pixelated woman tied

with a white rope to a black pole, her white
       sari embroidered with mud or blood. Nights

you were the *wax to seal what's unwritten—*
       the screen goes white in downdrifting light.

vii.

The screen goes white. In downdrifting light,
    the stairwell is a charred tunnel. We walk out
of it into the courtyard—my skirt flares a rent
    into the burnt evening. *Something was silent,*

something went its way—something gnashes
    inside me, sister—along the yellow gashes
of paint guiding me through these rooms lined
    with glass cases, past machine gun chains

shaped into the word *Bangla.* Here, on this
    stage, a dancer bows low her limbs
once more before us. The stage goes silent.
    We gather ourselves: souvenirs of bone.

Pray, Lord. We are near. Near are we, Lord—
    in a courtyard, in these stacks of chairs.

Many corpses are stacked, Mother once told me, *because there's no space.* The plot of land I bend my head over is impossibly green: vines and plants grown over the thatched bamboo of the other graves. Someone has planted a glossy-leafed sapling over Grandmother's grave: it gives against the strain of wind that carries with it a fresh rain that falls upon my clasped hands. I imagine the bodies stacked like the books, scarves, and notebooks filling the suitcase I'll wheel into the crowded airport. I imagine them pressed like flowers in a book, thinning over time under the weight of new bodies.

Aubade Ending with the Death of a Mosquito

—at Apollo Hospital, Dhaka

Let me break
                    free of these lace-frail
                    lilac fingers disrobing
the black sky
                    from the windows of this
                    room, I sit helpless, waiting,
silent—sister,
                    because you drew from me
                    the coil of red twine: loneliness—
spooled inside—
                    once, I wanted to say one
                    true thing, as in, *I want more*
in this life,
                    or, *the sky is hurt, a blue vessel*—
                    we pass through each other,
like weary
                    sweepers haunting through glass
                    doors, arcing across gray floors
faint trails
                    of dust we leave behind—he
                    touches my hand, waits for me
to clutch back
                    while mosquitoes rise like smoke
                    from this cold marble floor,
from altars,
                    seeking the blood still humming
                    in our unsaved bodies—he sighs,

I make a fist,
                I kill this one leaving raw
                kisses raised on our bare necks—
because I woke
                alone in the myth of one life, I will
                myself into another—how strange,
to witness
                nameless, the tangled shape
                our blood makes across us,
my open palm.

Dhaka Nocturne

I admit that when the falling hour
begins to husk the sky free of its
saffroning light, I reach for anyone

willing to wrap his good arm tight
around me for as long as the ribboned
darkness allows. Who wants, after all,

to be seen too clearly? Still, the heart
trusts, climbs back down the old
mango tree outside the bar to marvel

at the gymnast tornadoing forward,
electrifying the air with her soaring
body on the TV, even as the friend

beside me asks, *But how could you
sleep in the same room as your dead
sister's things?* Once, a man I loved

told me I was stunning. It terrified
me, the way grief still can, risen
above us in the bar, seeking its own

body. I tell her the body, exhausted,
does what it must, as it did then,
sutured itself to his, said, *I'll be*

yours forever, with all its secretive
creases turning steam in this heat-
flustered city, wet fever of the nape

of my neck chiffoned beneath his
lips galaxying across it. I do not tell
her about the shelves of porcelain-

cheeked dolls tarnished lavender by
falling light, the ebony abundance
of my mother's hair varnished blue

as she slid my sister's child's clothes
off the old wooden hangers, then back
on—but what else is mine, if not all

this strange beauty? *Look,* I said to him,
running my own hands down myself:
night-rinsed anaglyph of muscle

and bone held fast against everything
yet to plunder this or any twilight's
nameless and numinous unfurling.

Reading Willa Cather in Bangladesh

There were again things which seemed destined for her . . .

I would give it up: this heaviness
built of neither silence nor snow. I am

there, but here, back in Virginia, walking
through shadows of leaves imprinted damp

on gray sidewalks. I would look toward
their soil-etched wings, and curl away

from dim corners where shadows must
be rubbed away from mirrors, where a TV

might flicker with the figure of a woman
dressed in green reading the news aloud

from blue-inked pages. Daily, it is possible
to forget. I would give it up: the commotion

of wrought-iron windows looking out to fields
of tea and rice, the failed light pouring through.

I would turn from beggar hands pressed against
glass, their hungry and open mouths. I would

rather be here, pacing in a room papered with
shadows of bare oak limbs, than there, sitting

quietly in each dark room that holds its breath, waits
for the hum of a generator to light its cement walls.

En Route to Bangladesh,
Another Crisis of Faith

We pass over heavy shadows
of large clouds pinned to train cars

lined up like unused blocks
of colored chalk—red then green,

blue then orange—until we are
propelled higher, and the trains

are swallowed by these jagged
strictures of land that are no longer

sand nor rock nor water, but a child's
drawing instead—until the distant ocean

is the only fabric that fills this punched-
out plastic hole of a window—that is

the blue that falls over everything, that is
everything—blue on blue on blue—like the one

seam of light left always on the airplane ceiling
that the pale, plastic shades cannot shut away—

until that narrow vein of light is the only
belief left, a cream-thick ribbon across our eyes—

I struggled my way onto a packed bus. I became all that surged past the busy roadside markets humming with men pulling rickshaws heavy with bodies. A light breeze from the river was cool on our faces through the open windows. Eager passengers ran alongside us. The bus slowed down. A young man grabbed those arms, pulled them through. The moon filled the dust-polluted sky: a ripe, unsheathed lychee. It wasn't enough light to see clearly by, but I still turned my face toward it.